Landmarks

EXPLORING
Suburbs

Jonathan Baldwin

WAYLAND

Landmarks

EXPLORING **Inner Cities**
EXPLORING **Seaside Towns**
EXPLORING **Suburbs**
EXPLORING **Villages**

Cover: A milkman delivers milk on one of his rounds; a girl requests a bus to stop; and a suburban housing estate on the outskirts of Brighton.

Title page: A private housing estate in South Glamorgan, near Cardiff in Wales.

Contents page: A detatched house for sale.

Series editor: Katie Orchard
Designer: Tim Mayer
Production controller: Carol Stevens

First published in 1997 by Wayland Publishers Limited
61 Western Road, Hove
East Sussex, BN3 1JD, England

© Copyright Wayland Publishers Limited 1997

Find Wayland on the internet at:
http://www.wayland.co.uk

British Library Cataloguing in Publication Data
Baldwin, Jonathan
  Exploring suburbs. – (Landmarks)
  1. Suburbs – Juvenile literature
  I. Title II. Suburbs
  307.7'4

ISBN 0 7502 1961 0

Typeset by Mayer Media
Printed and bound in Italy by G. Canale S.p.A.

Picture acknowledgements::
City of Bath Council 39 (both) Mary Evans 8 (right), 9; Eye Ubiquitous: Paul Thompson *contents page*, 4, 6 (bottom), Steve Lindridge 8 (left), 9; Paul Thompson 11 (top), 18 (top), John Hulme 21, A.J.G. Bell 26 (top), Paul Thompson 28, Tim Hawkins 31 (left), Sarah Heath 31 (right), Paul Seheult 34 (top), 35 (bottom), Andy Butler 36 (top); Richard Greenhill 15; Robert Harding 7, Robert Francis 18 (bottom); Impact: Bruce Stevens *Title Page*, Simon Shepheard 5 (bottom), 12, Bruce Stevens 16 (top), Piers Cavendish 20, 25, Caroline Penn 24, Simon Shepheard 26 (bottom), Robert Eames 29, Francesca Yorke 34 (bottom), Piers Cavendish 37 (bottom), Mike McQueen 40, Piers Cavendish 42; Public Record Office, Northern Ireland 32; Tesco Photographic Unit 27 (bottom); Wayland Picture Library Angus Blackburn 5 (top), 10, 11 (bottom), Zak Waters *cover* (top), Angus Blackburn 14, 16 (bottom), 17 (top and bottom), Zul Mukhida 22, 23, 25 (top), 27 (top), Angus Blackburn 29 (top), 30, 33, 35 (top), Steve White-Thomson 38, Tim Woodcock 41, 43. The pie chart on page 36 was produced by Tim Mayer. The artwork on page 47 was produced by Peter Bull.

Contents

What is a Suburb?   4

People and Communities   8

Earning a Living   16

Suburban Schools   22

On the Move   26

Shopping and Entertainment   32

Changing Suburbs   38

How to Investigate a Suburb   42

Notes About this Book   44

Glossary   46

Books To Read   47

Index   48

What is a Suburb?

A suburb is an area usually found on the edge of a town or city. Suburbs tend to be residential areas, mainly made up of housing. They often have a few local shops and services, such as newsagents and schools, that are needed by people living in the area.

Suburbs can vary greatly in size. Some of them may be quite small, perhaps just four or five houses. Others may be huge and almost like towns themselves, with thriving communities. One of the biggest suburbs in the UK is Lower Earley in Berkshire. It is a suburb on the outskirts of Reading, with 6,500 houses and 20,000 people living there. Although Lower Earley has quite a large population, it only has a few basic shops and one pub.

Homes in modern suburban housing estates such as this one in the Midlands often have garages.

Most of the buildings in suburban settlements are modern and tend to look alike. Suburbs grow up quickly and buildings there are usually built at the same time, so there is not much variation in them. Unlike inner-city areas, there are few tall buildings in the suburbs. Suburban homes also often have gardens, so they feel more spacious.

Many people are choosing to leave inner-city areas, so suburbs have become very popular in the UK. Today, more people live in suburban areas than in any other type of settlement.

Above This man is mowing the lawn in his garden in an Edinburgh suburb.

Left In a London suburb, these people are waiting for a bus to take them and their shopping home.

5

How suburbs develop

There are several reasons why suburbs have grown up where they are. Towns and cities have always attracted large numbers of people looking for work in the various shops and businesses there. As the populations of these areas have grown, so has the need for more housing. With very little space in inner cities for new houses, homes have been built on the outskirts of these built-up areas.

A new suburb offers big gardens and modern houses. These houses all look very similar because they were built at the same time.

Often families choose to move out of heavily built-up areas to escape the bustle of people and traffic. The lack of space in inner-city areas means that buildings there have become taller. Many families have decided to move away from these crowded areas to quieter areas with more space. Many parents with young children feel that suburbs are safer and more pleasant areas to live in.

Not all suburbs are new. Many were built around 100 years ago, such as Moseley, just outside the centre of Birmingham. At that time Moseley grew up on the edge of the city. But this early suburban area has been swallowed up by Birmingham, which has continued to grow.

People and Communities

Until the Industrial Revolution, most people lived in the countryside and farmed the land. Many farmers started to use the land to rear sheep instead of crops. This meant that far fewer people were needed to work on the land. Many people were forced to leave farming and look for other work. Most of them came to work in the new industrial cities such as Manchester, Glasgow and Leeds. They found jobs in factories.

Below **Houses such as these in Sheffield were built very close to the factories. Notice the huge chimneys towering above the rooftops.**

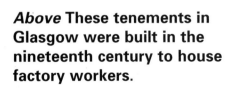

Above **These tenements in Glasgow were built in the nineteenth century to house factory workers.**

People working in factories needed to live close by, so their homes were built right next to them. In Glasgow, these workers' homes were called tenements. They were made up of small flats, each shared by a whole family of six or seven people. The tenements were very overcrowded. To make things worse, pollution from nearby factory chimneys was very bad for people's health.

Many people wanted a cleaner, more spacious environment in which to live and bring up their families. About a century ago, transport began to improve. Railways sprang up all over the UK and it became easier to travel from place to place. Wealthier people began to move away from the factories and the city centres, and catch the train to work. They had decided that it was worth the extra time and money it took to travel to work because they now enjoyed a better life in their new homes.

This Victorian lady is enjoying the space in the garden of her new suburban home.

Closer to the countryside

The new homes on the outskirts of the city were very different from the cramped housing in inner-city areas. Most of the new homes had gardens at the back and sometimes at the front as well. The houses were bigger, with more rooms, so people could have more privacy. By the end of the 1800s, many of these new houses had their own toilets and bathrooms inside the house. This was seen as a great luxury.

Large areas of open land were kept as parks for the people in these new houses to enjoy during their leisure time. The parks on the edges of towns made those areas feel more like the countryside. They became known as suburbs because they were seen as lying somewhere between the city (an urban area) and the countryside.

Many early suburban parks are still in use today. These children are getting ready to have a picnic in their local park.

Today, in areas such as Streatham, in south-west London, you can see what these suburbs, built nearly a hundred years ago, were like. The houses are quite large, with gardens, and many of the roads are tree-lined to make the area feel more rural. People living in Streatham, a London suburb, have plenty of open space, with Tooting Common and Streatham Common nearby.

Right **This tree-lined street in Southfields, London, was built in Victorian times.**

Above **One of the main attractions of living in the suburbs is having a garden. This man is making the most of his.**

Suburban homes

Suburbs have grown up round the edges of nearly all towns and cities in the UK. In many ways the houses are still very much the same as when they were first built. Quite a few of the houses are still detached or semi-detached. Often, houses in suburbs may look a bit like houses in rural areas because they have black and white patterns on the outside like some old country cottages do. They may sometimes be built with old-fashioned brick patterns on the outside to make them look older.

Since suburbs are mainly made up of housing, often there are not many other types of building. Although houses in

Activity

What is your idea of a perfect home? Think about what it would look like. How many rooms would it have? Would it have a garden? Design your ideal house and see how it compares with your classmates' designs.

This suburban housing estate has been designed to look like Tudor village housing.

suburbs built at the same time are usually similar, their owners often change them to suit their needs. Some owners may build on a new porch at the front or an extension on the side or back to give extra space. Over time, houses in suburbs may start to vary quite a bit.

Suburbs are continually changing to suit the needs of the people who live there. Newer suburbs sometimes include single-storey houses called bungalows, which some people find attractive. Many older people feel that this sort of home is a real advantage because it has no stairs.

CASE STUDY

Alan Drayton Way

Alan Drayton Way is a modern suburb just outside Bishopstoke, near Southampton, in Hampshire. It was built on farmland between 1978–1980. Alan Drayton Way is made up of about 500 three- and four- bedroomed houses, all with their own gardens and garages.

Within the suburb there are no other types of building apart from houses. Many of the roads only lead into the estate so there is little traffic. Often roads are called 'Close' or 'Way' rather than 'Street' or 'Road'.

Alan Drayton Way is a quiet place to live.

Most of the people who live in this suburb of Edinburgh are parents with small children.

The roads in many suburban areas are specially designed so that they only lead to the homes of the people who live there. These types of roads are called cul-de-sacs and tend to have far less traffic than ordinary roads. This means that there is less danger and noise from cars and it may be much safer for young children to play there.

SUBURBAN POPULATIONS	
Age in years	Percentage of people
0–14	29%
15–34	18%
35–59	46%
Over 60	7%

Who lives in a suburb?

Most houses in suburbs have about three or four bedrooms. This is because they have been designed for the use of families with children. Many young, single people find that a large suburban house is too expensive and too big for their needs. Elderly people whose children have grown up and left home often find that the average suburban house is larger than they need.

So many suburbs have large numbers of adults of working age with children who are at school.

Getting together

Not all groups of people enjoy living in suburban areas. Families without their own transport often find it difficult to reach the local town centre for some of the things that they need. Many young people feel that suburbs do not have so many interesting things for them to do. Many suburbs may, however, have youth clubs or community centres. Often suburban areas also have activity groups for young people such as Brownie or Scout packs. This can be a great way of building up a sense of community spirit. Brownie and Scout packs bring children and parents together on a regular basis. This can be very important if the suburb does not have its own school.

A pack of Brownies play together in a local park.

Earning a Living

People in the UK work in all sorts of different jobs, so it is sensible to group jobs together when we want to investigate them. It is usual to divide jobs into three different groups – primary, secondary and tertiary. People who work using natural materials, such as farmers growing food or miners digging for coal, are called primary workers. Others, who make goods out of natural products, such as people who make cars, are called secondary workers. Tertiary workers are people who provide a service, such as shop assistants or people who work in banks.

Above This window cleaner is providing a valuable service to people living in this suburb.

More and more people in the UK are moving away from primary and secondary jobs towards tertiary activity. A recent survey showed that 60% of all jobs in the UK are now in the tertiary sector.

Left This postwoman makes sure that people's mail is delivered safely and on time.

Providing a service

Since suburbs are mainly residential areas, there are few jobs within the suburbs themselves. Most people who work in suburbs are tertiary workers. They provide goods and services to people who live in the area. Local shops, found on small shopping parades, such as newsagents and grocers' shops, provide some jobs in suburban areas. Window cleaners, doctors and teachers also provide valuable services to people living locally. Local councils provide work for people such as refuse collectors and street cleaners. However, most people who live in suburbs tend to work some distance from their homes.

Above **A local newsagent is an important part of the community and also provides some jobs in the local area.**

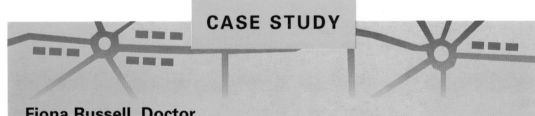

CASE STUDY

Fiona Russell, Doctor

Above **Fiona Russell makes a house call.**

Fiona Russell works in a busy doctor's surgery in the suburb of Cricklewood, on the outskirts of north London. Fiona can see up to thirty patients a day at the surgery, and then there are usually house calls to make.

When she is off duty, Fiona has to carry a bleeper to warn her if she is needed. When her bleeper goes off, Fiona drops what she is doing and rushes to the scene of the emergency.

'When my bleeper goes off, I don't always know what to expect before I get to the patient. I often have to think and act very quickly,' says Fiona.

17

The commuter belt

Since the 1930s, railway networks have snaked out all over the UK, linking towns and cities with suburbs and rural areas. This means that people who move away from the bustle of the cities to more peaceful areas can still keep their jobs in the cities. Today, millions of people living in suburbs in the UK are doing just that. They commute to work by car or public transport, and have very similar jobs to people who live in the cities. These commuters work in banks, businesses, hotels and restaurants.

Above Many people living in suburbs have to commute to towns and cities to get to work.

New businesses

Many businesses are now choosing to build outside the inner cities to beat the traffic and find more space. Huge factories have begun to open up away from city centres, providing many manufacturing, or secondary-sector jobs for people living in the surrounding areas. People living in nearby suburbs often find work in these new industries.

Right Many suburban workers have jobs in industrial areas on the outskirts of cities, such as this one near Reading.

Sam Marshall, Air Traffic Controller

Gatwick airport is always very busy.

Sam Marshall is an air traffic controller at Gatwick Airport. Sam monitors the movements of planes around Gatwick from the control tower. It is his job to make sure that all the planes around the airport are moving safely and on time.

Sam guides planes coming into Gatwick to make sure that they land safely. Planes are not allowed to move along the runways or take off until Sam tells them to.

'When weather conditions are bad, I have to keep calm because pilots are relying on me to guide them down,' says Sam.

In recent years, the large Japanese car manufacturer, Nissan, opened a big new factory in Sunderland. The factory provided a large number of jobs for people living in the area, including those living in the suburbs surrounding Sunderland and nearby Durham.

Most city airports are actually based just outside the city. Manchester Airport is situated south of Manchester. The airport provides a great variety of jobs for people living locally. Pilots, booking staff, mechanics, and restaurant workers are all needed to keep the airport running. Many of the people living in the suburb of Cheadle, just outside Manchester, have jobs at the airport.

Many major supermarkets have also moved to places that are a long way out of the city centre. This has provided lots of jobs for people who live in the suburbs nearby. Business parks and light industrial estates have also been built on vacant land on the edges of cities and towns, where it is easy for people who live in the suburbs nearby to reach them. Aztec West Business Park, built just north of Bristol, has been very successful. It is close to the motorway network, which allows commuters to get there from suburbs all over south-west England. Many businesses now wish to base themselves away from city centres, close to the main motorway routes.

This woman does not need to commute because she works from home.

Activity

To find out what sort of job the parents of pupils in your class do you could carry out a survey. You could do this by asking three simple questions:

1. Does the person work using natural materials, such as growing food, fishing or mining coal? (They work in the primary sector).
2. Does the person actually make goods, perhaps in a factory or workshop? (They work in the secondary sector).
3. Does the person provide a service to customers such as a shop assistant or a doctor? (They work in the tertiary sector).

For each person there should be only one 'Yes' answer (unless the person has two jobs!) You could present your findings in a table. It might then be useful to graph your results.

Working from home

Some people living in suburbs are finding it useful to work from home and so they cut out the need to travel to work altogether. These people can use a computer and a fax machine to work from their own homes. They are sometimes called tele-workers.

Unemployment

Not all suburbs offer good job opportunities. In some suburbs based around the UK's larger cities, unemployment may be a serious problem. During the 1980s, in Wood End, on the outskirts of Coventry, unemployment was very high. Many young people had very little to do and became bored. Windows were broken and graffiti sometimes was drawn on bus shelters and walls. In the late 1980s, more money was put into the suburb and a new community centre was built to give young people something to do. Some new houses were also built to encourage young families into the area.

This man is checking the latest job vacancies at the job centre.

Suburban Schools

Schools in suburban areas are not very different from schools in other types of settlements. A school day is very much the same in most areas in the UK, with lessons, playtimes and lunch breaks. But unlike in an inner city, most children who go so suburban schools usually live no more than twenty minutes away.

Just as suburbs can vary a lot in size, so can the size of their schools. Most suburban schools have been built at roughly the same time as the housing in the area. Whilst some village schools may only have about fifty children, most suburban schools might have between 150–400 pupils. Planners deciding where to build the houses in an area take a careful look at the number of children that are likely to live there. This information helps them to plan the number of schools and places that are needed for pupils.

This junior school in a suburb of Peacehaven, in East Sussex, has modern buildings and plenty of space for the children to play.

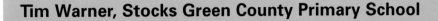

Tim Warner, Stocks Green County Primary School

Tim Warner is ten years old. He goes to Stocks Green County Primary School in a suburb of Tonbridge in Kent. The school was built in the 1960s at the same time as the houses around it.

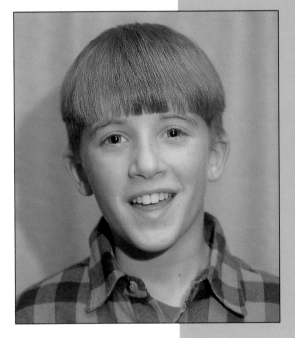

Tim lives in a quiet cul-de-sac near the school and cycles there and back along special cycle routes. The school has a place where Tim and his friends can leave their bicycles during the day.

Tim's school is medium-sized, serving about 200 children. There are seven classes, from Year One to Year Six. The school has large playing fields, which Tim uses to play football. There is also a 'wild area', which has been set aside for school nature projects.

'I really like the new wild area. We use it for science, art and geography. It's fun to have some lessons outside,' says Tim.

School buildings

Suburban schools can have quite a few advantages. Often a school in the suburbs has modern buildings with plenty of space. There might also be special areas within the school building for modern equipment, such as computers. Many suburban schools have lots of open space, and have large playing fields. Some suburban schools, such as Westergate Primary School in West Sussex, have a special 'wild area', where the children can study nature and the environment.

Being between the city and the countryside means that many suburban schools have the advantages of both types of settlement. Suburban children can make trips to the nearest city or town to visit the theatre, museums or art galleries quite easily. They can also go out into rural areas for field trips without having to travel too far.

A part of the community

Suburban schools provide a very important focus for the local community. Many parents may be closely linked to the school through a 'Parent-Teacher Association'. They can help organize events and raise money for special items that the school badly needs.

Not all suburban schools are new. Highgate Junior School, in North London was built in the 1950s.

Activity

Using a large-scale map of your school area you can find out how far pupils travel to get to your school.

Find where you and your classmates live on the map. Use different coloured dots to mark where each of you lives. Using the map scale, work out the distance from each dot to the school. Use a piece of string to follow the twists and turns of the roads to find out the exact distances. Plot your findings on a graph. What is the average distance?

As most suburban schools were built quite recently, often the area around the school has been planned with safety in mind. Some children may cycle to school, so cycle lanes are often provided to keep them safe from traffic. Pedestrian crossings and footbridges can also keep traffic and children at a safe distance from each other.

Children from Dragon School on the outskirts of Oxford take part in the school's sports day.

On the Move

Good transport networks are extremely important in suburban areas. The people who live there need to be able to reach shops and services easily. Most people who live in suburbs also have to commute to their place of work. So having access to a good network of roads, trains and buses is essential.

Above **People living in Manchester's suburbs rely on buses such as this one to travel into the city centre.**

Trains

At the end of the nineteenth century the UK had a very good railway system. This allowed suburbs to develop around railway stations on the edges of towns and cities. The suburb of Mottingham, in south-east London, grew up around the railway station there. Railways gave the people who lived in suburbs easy access to the city centre and its jobs. In London a system of underground railways was built. This helped people to travel easily from the suburbs to their place of work.

Right **Every day in London, thousands of people use the Underground to commute from the suburbs to the inner city.**

Buses

Many people living in suburbs rely on local bus services to take them to and from the city. But in some suburbs, buses may not come very often or there may be no public transport at all. Some groups of people, such as parents with young children, or elderly people, can find it very difficult to get out and about if they do not have their own transport. As a response to this problem, some large, out-of-town stores offer a free bus service to their main branches.

Although car ownership is increasing, many people still depend on buses to travel.

CASE STUDY

The driver of Tesco's free bus service waits to take shoppers back home.

Tesco's Free Bus Service

When the Tesco supermarket in Chichester first opened in September 1993, a free bus service was offered to all their customers. Since then, the service has been very successful.

Every day, except for bank holidays and Sundays, buses leave the branch every fifteen minutes and drive around the outskirts of Chichester to bring people to the supermarket.

Many people living in the surrounding suburbs rely on the bus service to get into town. The service is particularly popular with the elderly, schoolchildren, and parents with young children.

People who use the service find that it is very helpful, especially those who don't have cars of their own.

Cars

Over the last fifty years, many commuters have moved away from using trains and buses. Car ownership is becoming much more common. Some families now may have more than one car. Modern suburbs need to be able to cope with the increase in the numbers of cars on the roads.

A modern suburb needs to be easy to reach by car because that is how most people living there travel. Sometimes a road has to be built specially so that a new suburb can be linked to other roads in the area. The growth in the number of car users in the UK has led to a need for bigger roads, such as motorways, which can carry them.

CAR OWNERSHIP
Nottingham can give us some clues about car ownership in the suburbs. In the suburb of Lowdham, 25% of families have two or more cars, 53% have one car and only 22% have no car. But in the Park area of the inner city, 55% have no car.

Planners now recognize that most people living in suburban areas use a car. These new houses in the Midlands all have garages.

Even motorways are so busy that often they cannot cope with all the traffic. It was recently proposed to increase the M25 around London to twelve lanes in each direction.

Motorways allow people to travel long distances quickly. For this reason, some people are able to live a long way from where they work. The M4 runs from London to Bristol and all along it in towns such as Reading, Newbury and Swindon, new suburbs have been built. Some people are worried as they feel that the suburbs are growing too quickly, and that large areas of countryside are being swallowed up by new housing and roads. In Berkshire, 10,000 new homes are needed by the year 2000 but people cannot agree about where they should be built as there is very little space available.

Many commuters living on the outskirts of Stafford rely on the M6 motorway to get them to and from work.

Activity

Conduct a survey of your friends and find out which method of transport they use to get to school. Make a note of the different types of transport and note how many of your friends use each type. Put your results in a table to see which is the most common method of transport.

As more and more people have come to rely on their cars, even for short journeys, many suburbs have begun to experience problems with traffic congestion. During the rush hour, when people are travelling to and from work, huge traffic jams can build up. To help solve this problem, many local councils are thinking about improving public transport to make it more attractive to car owners. The aim is to encourage more people to leave their cars at home.

Above **These ramps on the road help to slow down traffic.**

Above **Cycle lanes help to keep cyclists safe from lorries and cars.**

With so many cars on suburban roads, safety is something that concerns many people. In some suburban areas, cycle lanes have been set up to try and keep cyclists safe from other vehicles. Pelican crossings can help keep pedestrians safe from cars. In some suburbs, traffic-calming measures have been tried, such as ramps or narrow points in a road. These force cars to drive more slowly through suburban areas.

Shopping and Entertainment

This Victorian family, living in a suburb in Northern Ireland, had to make its own entertainment.

In the past, people's leisure time might have been spent making their own entertainment, often in the home. About 100 years ago, some families used to gather around a piano to sing popular songs of the day. Children used to make their own toys from bits and pieces they found around the house. People would also go out to watch plays and listen to concerts.

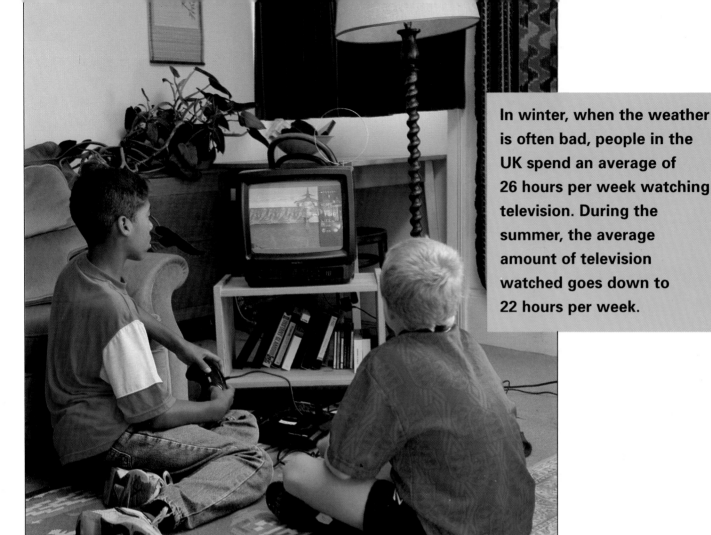

In winter, when the weather is often bad, people in the UK spend an average of 26 hours per week watching television. During the summer, the average amount of television watched goes down to 22 hours per week.

These children have settled down to play a computer game.

Modern technology

More recently, television has had a huge effect on the way people spend their leisure time. In the UK today, over 95 per cent of all households have a television. In many large suburban homes there may be more than one television. Many children and young people have a television in their own room so that they can watch what they want.

New technology has also bought the video, music systems and, perhaps most important of all, the computer into many homes, including those in the suburbs. The computer provides people with various kinds of entertainment without even going outside their front door.

Gardens

Many suburban homes have gardens where children can play safely. Large suburban homes may also have their own leisure facilities, such as small swimming-pools. In many suburbs the summer can be a good time for friends to meet for a barbecue in the garden.

Getting out of the house

Some of the largest open areas for recreation in suburbs are the local school playing fields. These can often be used by the community after school hours and at weekends for games, such as football. Some schools, usually large

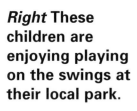

Above Many suburban gardens have enough room for a barbecue in the summer.

Right These children are enjoying playing on the swings at their local park.

secondary schools, have their own leisure centres which are used by the pupils in the daytime and the whole community at the weekend and in the evenings. These schools are known as community colleges.

Suburbs usually have good access to leisure centres built on the outskirts of towns or cities. A leisure centre can be a good focus for the suburban community because people can meet and talk there as well as take part in the activities offered.

Above Team sports, such as football, can be an important focus for young people living in suburban areas.

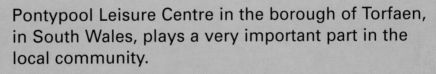

CASE STUDY

Pontypool Leisure Centre

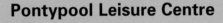

Pontypool Leisure Centre in the borough of Torfaen, in South Wales, plays a very important part in the local community.

The centre provides many different sports facilities for people of all ages and abilities. As well as keep-fit and martial arts classes, there are also squash and badminton courts. The swimming-pools and giant water tubes are especially popular with visitors.

Pontypool Leisure Centre even has a children's room so parents can use the sports facilities while their children are looked after. There is a special hall for concerts, shows and exhibitions.

Above Water tubes can be great fun.

35

Local shops

For many people, shopping is an important leisure activity. When suburbs were built, sometimes a small group of shops was included in the plans. This is called a shopping parade. These small shopping areas provide local people with many different services. The shopping parade in Cradlehall Park, a suburb of Inverness, in Scotland, has a doctor's surgery, a baker's shop, and an a twenty-four-hour shop.

N
E
S
W

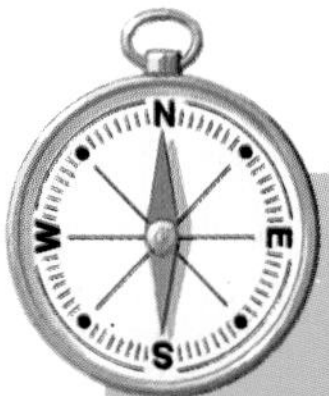

Activity

How much spare time do you have, and how do you spend it? To find out, draw a circle and divide it into 24 equal parts. Each section shows one hour. Mark 12 am at the top of the circle and 12 pm at the bottom. You can then divide the circle to show how you spend your time. Give each activity a colour, and draw a key. It is up to you if you choose a weekday or the weekend, as they will be very different.

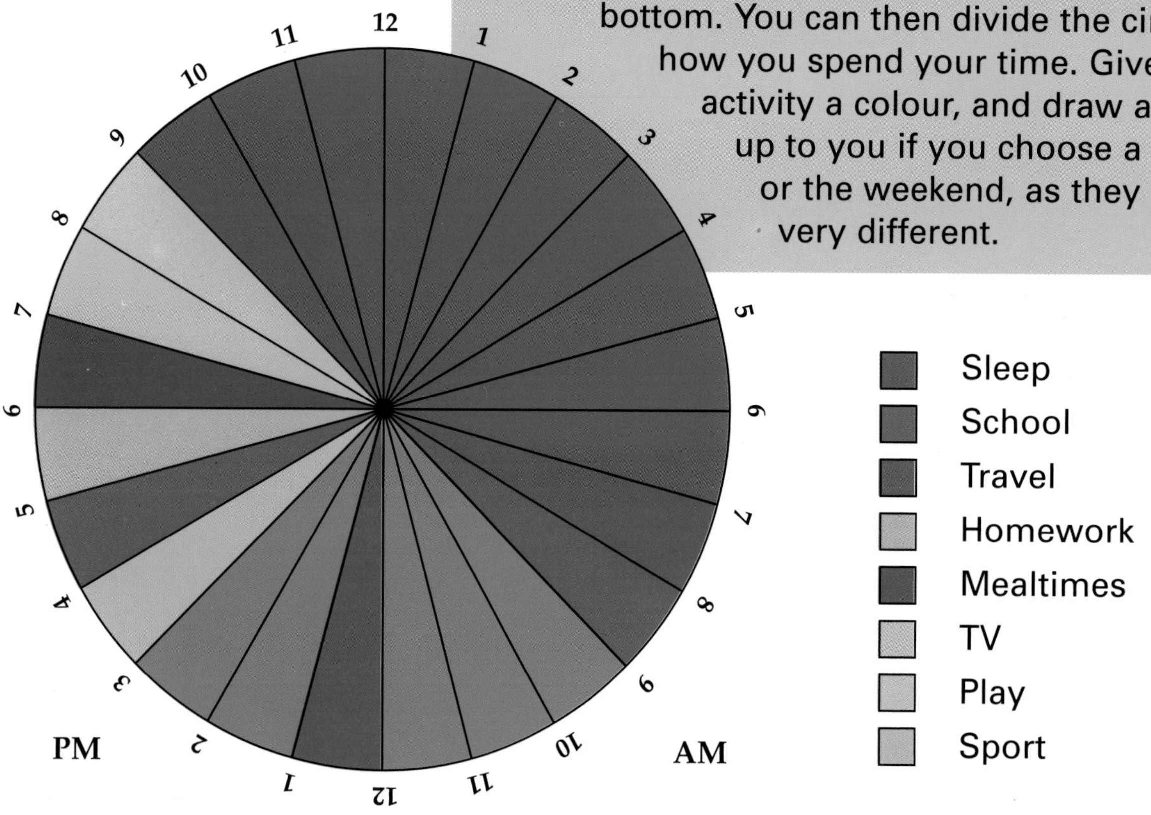

12
1
2
3
4
5
6
7
8
9
10
11
12
11
10
9
8
7
6
5
4
3
2
1
AM
PM
Sleep
School
Travel
Homework
Mealtimes
TV
Play
Sport

Today, many people have stopped using these local shops because they now shop at large, out-of-town shopping complexes. These shopping complexes sell a large range of goods, from food and sports equipment, to clothes and furniture. Many people living in suburban areas prefer to shop at large complexes because they can do all of their shopping in one place. This means that more of their time can be spent on other leisure activities. Quite often, these complexes also have cafés and restaurants. Some of the larger shopping centres, such as Clydebank Shopping Centre, on the outskirts of Glasgow, even have cinemas.

Smaller suburban shopping parades have found it very difficult to compete against the large new complexes. Many specialist local shops have been forced to shut down because they no longer have enough customers.

Above **This modern parade of shops provides useful services for people living in the Hampden Park area of Eastbourne.**

Left **Large, new shopping complexes can afford to offer lower prices, so smaller local shops are having to close down.**

37

Changing Suburbs

Suburbs are pleasant places to live in, away from the noise and pollution of inner-city areas. But even so, local councils do need to think of the future. Suburbs, just like every other kind of settlement, are constantly changing to suit the needs of the people who live there. Planners need to think about the balance beween keeping the good things about living in a suburb, and making changes to improve it.

In 1984, there were only 2,144 bottle bank sites in the UK. By 1994, there were 12,858!

Going green

One growing problem in the UK is that of litter. This can affect many suburban areas. One way that people might improve the environment, as well as saving resources, is by recycling paper, glass and cans. Many supermarkets now have special areas where people can take glass, paper and cans to be collected. Some shopping parades also have recycling sites.

Growing suburbs

With more and more people choosing to live away from towns and cities, many people are worried about losing green areas to make way for new housing. To stop suburbs spreading too far, some areas around a city or town cannot be built on and must be kept as open countryside. These areas are called 'Green Belts', because they are still covered in fields and trees.

Recycling bins are becoming a more and more common sight on our streets.

Bath's Green Boxes

In and around the city of Bath, the charity Friends of the Earth and the local council have formed a partnership to boost the amount of household waste that is recycled.

Each home in the area is provided with a special 'Green Box' to put glass and cans in. People are encouraged to put other types of waste, such as paper, foil and clothing in separate bags on top of the boxes.

The recyclable waste is then collected on a weekly basis by specially designed vehicles with separate cages for different types of waste. The waste is then easily removed with a fork-lift truck. In 1995, 3,500 tonnes of bottles, cans and newspapers were recycled by the scheme. This meant that 25 per cent of all waste in the area was recycled!

Above These people are sorting out bottles from cans and other types of waste.

Right This fork-lift truck takes the waste from the van to be recycled.

39

Traffic congestion

Traffic congestion in our suburbs is a growing problem. By law now, each local council in the UK now has to think of a plan to reduce the number of cars on the roads. One way is to encourage people to leave their cars at home. Alternative methods of transport are being promoted, with plans for new cycle and bus lanes. This has the added advantages of reducing pollution and improving road safety. Public transport needs to be improved so that it is more attractive, even to car owners. At the moment the number of cars looks as if it will continue to rise and traffic jams will be a problem well into the next century.

New suburban houses are being built every day to cope with people wanting to move out of the inner cities. These new houses are on the outskirts of Leicester.

More people may start to work from home using a computer and fax, freeing them from the need to commute at all. This could also mean fewer cars on the road.

Suburban communities are now looking to the future and are really working hard to improve their environment.

These children have a safe place to play outside their homes.

Activity

One way of comparing different parts of the area you live in is to do an Environmental Quality Survey. Decide on a list of things that you think are important, such as litter and noise. Give each item a score out of ten using the key below:

SCORE (1–10)

1. LITTER
    1 = Lots of litter
    10 = No litter to be seen at all

2. PAVEMENTS
    1 = Lots of broken paving with pot holes
    10 = Perfectly smooth surface

3. TRAFFIC SAFETY
    1 = No safe paths and lots of traffic
    10 = Traffic and pedestrians kept apart

4. NOISE
    1 = Very high levels of noise
    10 = Very quiet and pleasant

5. BUILDING CONDITION
    1 = Buildings in bad condition
    10 = All buildings in very good condition

You can add the score together to get a score out of 50. You could conduct your survey outside your school, at the local shops and near your home, and see which area gets the highest score.

How to Investigate a Suburb

There are many ways to start investigating a suburb. Below are some ideas for you to consider as a starting point for your research.

First-hand information
Local churches or community halls sometimes have notices describing events in an area. Many shops and small supermarkets also have a place where people can put up notices. Local newspapers include interesting news items about daily life in a suburb. The letters page will show you what people think about future plans for the area.

People in the know
Parents, teachers, relatives and neighbours are likely to have visited or lived in suburban areas. Try talking to them about their experiences. Many of the older local people may remember what the suburb was like when it was first built. They may even have some old photographs that you can look at.

Local libraries can sometimes provide information about suburban areas. The reference section is particularly useful. The librarian will help you to find census information, Ordnance Survey maps, books, encyclopaedias, magazines and newspapers.

The planning departments of some local councils can also send you information about future plans for the area, along with facts and figures.

Maps

There are a variety of maps to look at when studying a suburb. An A–Z-style street map will show you all the local roads, green areas, important buildings and stations. An Ordnance Survey map will give you all this in much more detail. Large-scale maps of a suburb can help you pinpoint changes in the area which show how the suburb has grown.

Census information

Census information shows us how particular areas have changed over the years, and what they are like now. The information includes the numbers of people living in an area and their ages, whether they are single, married or divorced, where they were born, whether they are working, unemployed or retired, what kind of housing they live in and whether or not they own a car. You can find census information in a large public library.

Places to visit

Local libraries or planning departments of local councils often have old maps of the area that you can compare with modern ones to see how the area has developed. Parks and buildings in an area often give clues to the age of a suburb.

Collecting and presenting your evidence

Collect all the information you find, such as leaflets, bus or train tickets, photocopies of maps, and newspaper cuttings, and design your own suburban scrapbook or poster promoting the area. Think about using other types of media, such as CD-ROM encyclopaedias, photographs or tape recordings of interviews. Also, if you have access to a computer, you could enter your findings on a database.

Notes About this Book

The main text in each book in the Landmarks series provides general information about four types of settlement within the contexts of communities, work, schools, transport, shopping and entertainment, and change. Each book in the series features the same areas of study so that the four different types of settlements can be compared easily with each other within a general context.

Case studies give specific information about a particular aspect of each chapter and sometimes provide direct quotes from people who live and work in different kinds of settlements. Students can use this information to make a direct comparison with their own experience.

The activities are designed so that children from any type of settlement can do them. They can be used to demonstrate what the main text has already stated about the locality mentioned in the book, or as a contrast. Throughout the series children are encouraged to work with the various tools that a geographer uses to study a particular area, such as mapping and graph skills, conducting surveys and using primary source evidence such as census material.

What is a Suburb? (pages 4–7)
This chapter gives a brief outline of the different types of suburbs found in the UK. The language and examples have been designed to encourage children to look around them, and either compare or contrast their own settlement with that of a suburb. The text examines what special features distinguish suburbs from other types of settlement.

Activity on page 6:
Looking at the types of buildings found in a settlement gives us clues as to the history of the area. An area mainly made up of housing is probably quite new. Old buildings may now be used for a purpose other than what they were originally built for.

People and Communities (pages 8–15)
In this chapter children are encouraged to look at the kinds of people living in a suburb, its key buildings and focal points of suburban life.

Activity on page 12:
This activity encourages children to think about what features of where they live are important to them. Ask them to think about where their ideal home would be situated, and whether or not it would have a garden or garage. What sorts of facilities would they need to have near their ideal home?

Earning a Living (pages 16–21)
This chapter deals with the kinds of jobs people do within suburbs. Children are encouraged to think about how the nature of a suburban settlement affects the types of employment found there.

Activity on page 20:
This exercise should help to provide a picture of the nature of work within a settlement. What percentage of the people questioned work in the tertiary sector?

Suburban Schools (pages 22–25)
This chapter allows children to compare or contrast their school with suburban examples illustrated in the text.

Activity on page 25:
This simple mapping activity encourages children to think about the distances that an average pupil has to travel to get to school. The activity also gives a very visual idea of the catchment area of the school.

On the Move (pages 26–31)
This chapter explains the importance of good transport networks in and around suburban areas, and the environmental implications of modern forms of transport.

Activity on page 30:
This activity looks at methods of transport used by the children. Do most children travel to school by car, or do they live near enough to walk? Find out how many of the children's families have cars, even if they don't need them to get to school.

Shopping and Entertainment (pages 32–37)
This chapter shows how the character of a suburb is reflected in the local shops and facilities, and how these have changed.

Activity on page 36:
This activity encourages children to think about how much of their day is spent doing leisure activities. Ask them to notice how much time they spend watching television. If you have access to a computer it might be fun to produce the information as a pie chart or a graph.

Change and the Future: (pages 38–41)
Whilst suburban settlements are attractive places to live, the changing way of life can bring problems, which need to be resolved.

Activity on page 41:
This activity encourages children to think about their local environment. Which areas scored lowest in the survey? Ask the children to think about what could be done to improve the worst areas.

Glossary

Business parks Areas outside towns or cities, where new factory units have been built.

Census A survey carried out every ten years in the UK to find out how many people live in the UK, where they live, and their way of life.

Commute Travel some distance to get to work.

Congestion When a road becomes blocked up.

Detached Houses which are not joined together.

Estate An area of land with modern houses planned and built on it.

Extensions Extra parts of a house that are built on to make it bigger.

Industrial Revolution The time during the eighteenth and early nineteenth century when the development of new machinery led to the growth of factories in the UK.

Networks Patterns of roads that fit together so that people can move from one place to another.

Pedestrian crossings Safe areas to cross on roads.

Planners People who make plans for the development of a locality, usually working for the local county council.

Redundant When a worker is not needed any longer.

Residential area An area mainly made up of housing.

Rural In the countryside.

Semi-detached Houses joined on one side only.

Settlement A place where people live.

Traffic calming Features of roads which have been specially designed to slow down the flow of traffic.

Urban A word to describe a very densely populated settlement.

Books To Read

Britain by David Flint, (Wayland, 1996)

Homes (See for Yourself series) by Jeff Stanfield, (Wayland, 1997)

Kids' Britain by Betty Jerman, (Macmillan Children's Books, 1995)

Street (See for Yourself series) by Jeff Stanfield, (Wayland, 1997)

The United Kingdom by David Flint, (Simon and Schuster, 1992)

This map shows the main towns and cities whose suburbs are mentioned in this book, and the regional capitals.

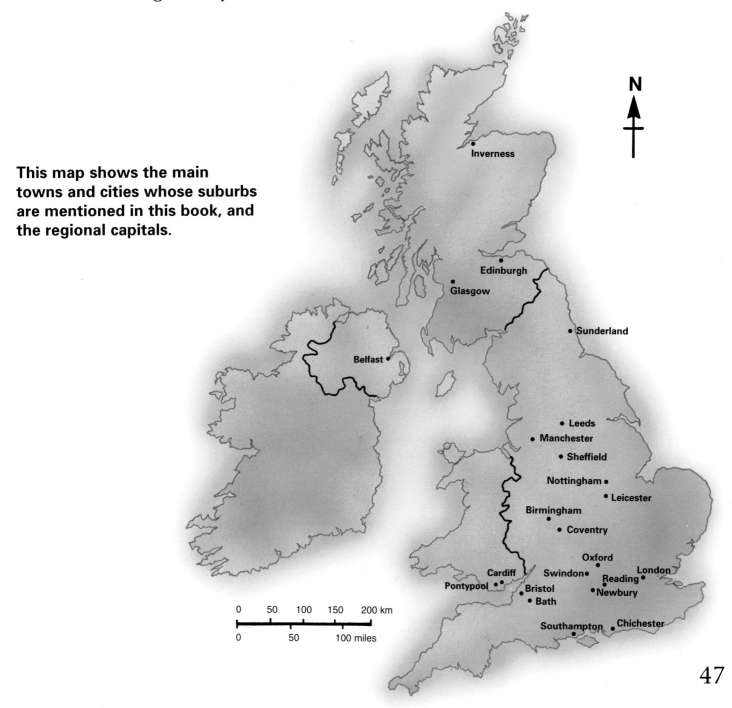

N

Inverness

Edinburgh

Glasgow

Sunderland

Belfast

Leeds

Manchester

Sheffield

Nottingham

Leicester

Birmingham

Coventry

Oxford

Cardiff

Swindon

London

Pontypool

Reading

Bristol

Newbury

Bath

Southampton

Chichester

| 0 | 50 | 100 | 150 | 200 km |

| 0 | 50 | 100 miles |

Index

airports 19

Bath 39
Birmingham 7
Brighton 6
Bristol 20, 29
businesses 6, 7, 18, 20

census 43
Chichester 27
community centres 15, 21, 42
commuters 18, 20, 26, 28
  tele-workers 21
computers 21, 23, 33, 40, 43
councils 17, 31, 38, 39, 40, 43
countryside 10, 24, 29, 38
Coventry 21
cul-de-sacs 14, 23

Edinburgh 5

factories 8, 9, 18, 19

garages 13, 28, 29
gardens 5, 10, 11, 13, 34
Glasgow 8
'Green-belt areas' 38

Hampden Park 36
housing 4, 6, 8, 10, 11, 12, 13, 14, 22, 29, 38
  bungalows 13
  detached 12
  extensions 13

flats 9, 10
  high-rise 6
  housing estates 6
  semi-detached 12
  tenements 9

industrial estates 20
Industrial Revolution 8–9
inner cities 5, 6, 7, 10, 18, 22, 29, 38
Inverness 36

jobs 4, 16–21, 26
  primary sector 16, 20
  secondary sector 16, 18, 19, 20
  tertiary sector 16, 17, 19, 20

Leeds 8
Leicester 40
leisure centres 35
London 5, 11, 26, 28, 29, 31

Manchester 8, 19, 26
motorways 20, 28, 29

Newbury 29
Northern Ireland 32
Nottingham 29

Oxford 24

parks 10, 43
Peacehaven 22
planners 22, 42, 43
playing fields 23, 34, 35
pollution 9, 40

Pontypool 35
population 4, 6, 15

Reading 4, 29
recycling 38–39

schools 4, 14, 15, 22–25, 30, 34–5
Sheffield 37
shops 6, 16, 17, 26, 36, 41, 42
  shopping complexes 37
  shopping parades 17, 36, 37, 38
  supermarkets 20, 27, 37, 38, 42
Southampton 13
Sunderland 19
Swindon 29

technology 33
television 33
traffic 7, 14, 25, 28, 40, 41
transport 9, 15, 18, 26, 27–31, 40
  buses 26, 27, 40
  cars 18, 19, 28, 29, 31, 40
  cycling 23, 25, 31, 40
  railways 9, 18, 26
  Underground railways 26

unemployment 21

Victorian times 8, 9, 32